# Life in Viking Times

## Samantha Skyrme

**Colourpoint**

## The Author

Samantha Skyrme received her MA in Scandinavian Studies at Edinburgh University, where she also learnt both Danish and Old English. She has worked in the Ulster Museum on the museum's collection of Dark Age axe heads.

At special sessions, she has taught the subject of the Vikings to P6 children in schools.

Samantha is a member of the National Association of Writers in Education, the Society of Authors and its Educational Writers' Group. She is also a member of the English Companions, an Anglo-Saxon society.

ISBN  1 898392 24 2

© Samantha Skyrme
1998

**Illustrator:  Vinko Kalcic**

**(except page 9: John Brogan)**

## Acknowledgments

National Museum of Ireland  28 (lower left), 34, 37 (coin), 52 (both), 57 (top right).
Hulton Getty Images  33.
The Viking Ship Museum, Roskilde  16 (both), 17
York Archaeological Trust  Cover, 11 (skate), 24, 26, 28 (top and lower right), 36, 40 (lower), 41, 43, 48, 49 (both), 55, 57 (lower).
© Crown Copyright. Reproduced with the permission of the Controller of Her Majesty's Stationery Office: 7 (both), 23 (lower).
Norman Johnston  56 (high cross).
By kind permission of the City of Bayeux  60.

**Colourpoint Books**

**Unit D5, Ards Business Centre**
**Jubilee Road**
**NEWTOWNARDS**
**Co Down**
**BT23 4YH**

**Tel:  01247 820505 (direct) or 819787 ext 239**
**Fax: 01247 821900**
**E-mail: info@colourpoint.co.uk**
**Web site: www.colourpoint.co.uk**

The publisher would like to acknowledge the invaluable help and advice given by Maurice Todd during the production of this book. His knowledge, both of the subject and of children, has greatly enhanced the publication.

# Contents

PAGE 3

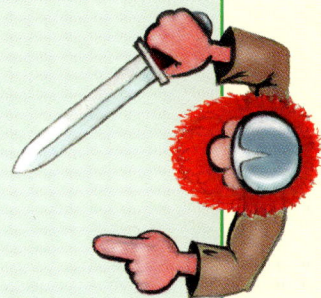

# Your long journey back in time!

This is a story of life long, long ago.

It starts in the eighth century, when life was very different from the way it is today.

# Timeline

**1066 The Battle of Hastings**
**The Normans invade England**

**1014**
**The Battle of Clontarf**

**1002**
**Brian Boru becomes High King of Ireland**

**917**
**Vikings begin to live in Dublin**

**795**
**First Viking attack on Ireland at Rathlin Island**

**871**
**Alfred the Great becomes king of the Saxons in England**

**866**
**York, in England, captured by the Vikings**

**793**
**First Viking attack on Britain.**
**Start of the Viking age**

**410 AD**
**The Romans leave Britain**

# Life in the eighth century

In the eighth century most people lived and worked on farms.

They lived in round houses made of timber or wattle-and-daub. These houses had thatched roofs.

The house was surrounded by a circular wall which protected it from any attack. People often got into fights with their neighbours, so it was important to protect their houses from attack.

**wattle and daub, thatched.**

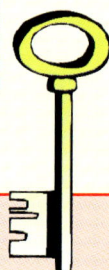

# Life in a monastery

Other people decided to live a holy life. Men could become **monks** and live in **monasteries**. Women could become **nuns** and in live in **convents**.

Many years ago, archaeologists found the ruins of a monastery at **Nendrum**, on an island in Strangford Lough in Northern Ireland. This monastery was built soon after St Patrick had been to Ireland.

The top picture was taken from an aeroplane and shows what it looks like today. The bottom picture shows what an artist thinks it might have looked like when the Vikings came.

Look at the pictures of Nendrum. Talk about what you can still see in the ruins and what the artist thinks it used to look like. Can you see the round tower?

Many things have disappeared. Why do you think this is?

**monk, monastery, nun, convent, raided.**

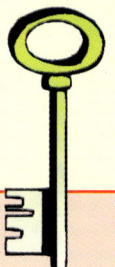

Life in a monastery or a convent was tough. The monks and nuns had to follow strict rules and worked hard all day.

## The monks spent their time...

... reading, learning, painting and drawing.

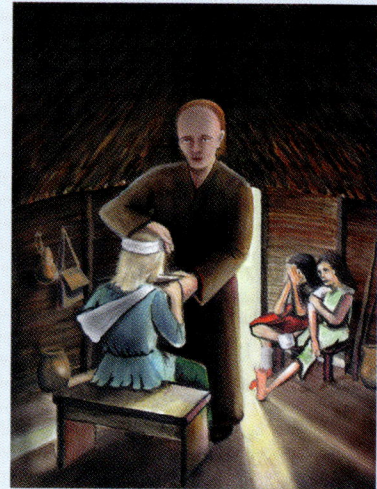

... nursing the sick.

... looking after the animals and working in the fields.

... praying and singing hymns.

If you lived in a monastery or convent, which job would you like best?

# Strangers arrived from across the sea

Then strangers arrived from across the sea and everything changed.

These strangers were called **Vikings**.

**Think about this picture.**

What kind of person would you need to be to survive these journeys across the sea? What skills would you need?

Could *you* have done it?

Why is the man carrying an axe?

What do you think the red and yellow things are at the bottom of the picture?

# What was a Viking?

The Vikings were **invaders**, **settlers** and **traders**.

They came from the Scandinavian countries of Denmark, Norway and Sweden.

Scandinavia is in the far north of Europe. There was a lot of competition for land for farming.

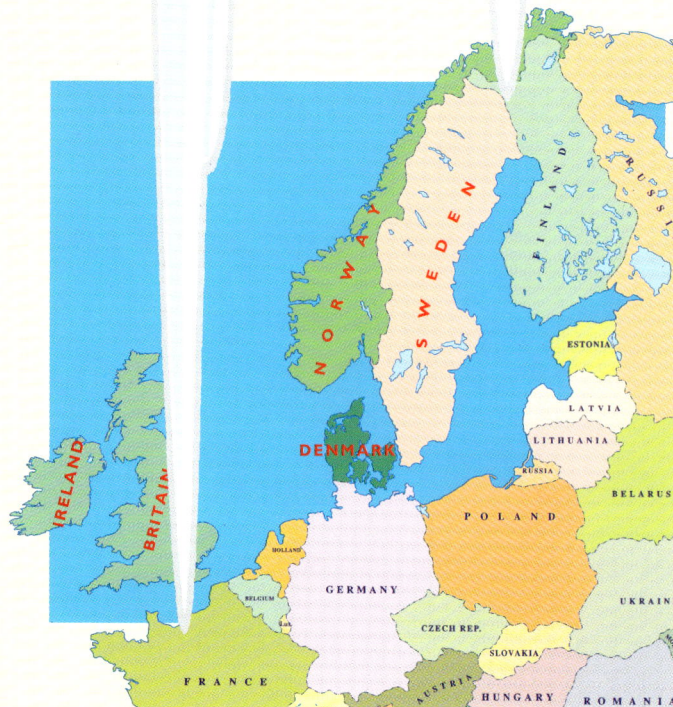

The Vikings left their own countries because their lands were very cold and there was not enough food for everyone to eat.

The Vikings began to arrive in Britain and Ireland in the 790s. You can see this on the timeline at the start of the book.

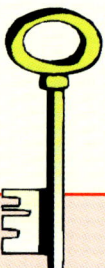

**invader, settler, trader, competition.**

# Travelling in Scandinavia

The centre of Norway and Sweden is made up of mountains. There are also forests, bogs, lakes and rivers. In the time of the Vikings, travelling overland was very difficult. It was often easier to travel by water.

In the winter, lakes and rivers froze and the snows came down. It then became easier to travel across land using snow shoes, skis, or toboggans.

The Vikings also had skates. They would skate along rivers or across lakes. This is a picture of a real Viking skate. Archaeologists found it at York, in England. The blade was made of bone.

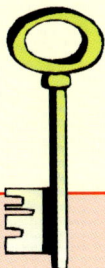

**toboggan.**

A real Viking once wore this skate. Can you make up a story about this person, and how the skate came to be lost? The person could be a man or a woman, or even a child.

# Erik the Red and Greenland

**Erik the Red** was a Viking. He was sent away from Norway because he had murdered someone.

He was sent to **Iceland**, but he did not stay there very long. He murdered some more people and was sent away from there for three years.

Erik spent this time exploring the west coast of **Greenland.** He called the country Greenland because he hoped the name would encourage people to come to live there.

At the end of the three years he went back to Iceland where he persuaded other people to come and live in Greenland with him.

What he *didn't* tell them was that most of Greenland was covered in ice and snow!

**encourage, persuade, settle.**

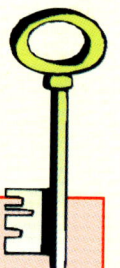

In the year 985 Erik set off across the sea with twenty-five ships full of families that wanted to settle in Greenland. Only fourteen of these ships made it as far as Greenland. The other ships sank in rough weather during the journey.

Describe the weather conditions in the picture on page 12.

Describe the weather conditions in the picture on page 13.

Describe the feelings of the people on the ships in each picture.

Imagine your family is going to Greenland with Erik the Red. Write about your feelings. Here are some words you might use:

**friends, scared, food, sea, trust, ships, pet, mother, father, excited.**

# The Vikings discovered America

The Vikings even got as far as **America**. They were the first Europeans to make it across the Atlantic Ocean to America. The Vikings first saw it in 985, but no one tried to settle there until the year 1000.

The Vikings called America 'Vinland'. This name meant 'Wine Land'.

**Why do you think they called America 'Vinland'?**

# How did the Vikings get here?

The Vikings came across the sea in powerful boats which we call **longships**. Longships were built of oak. They could be sailed or rowed.

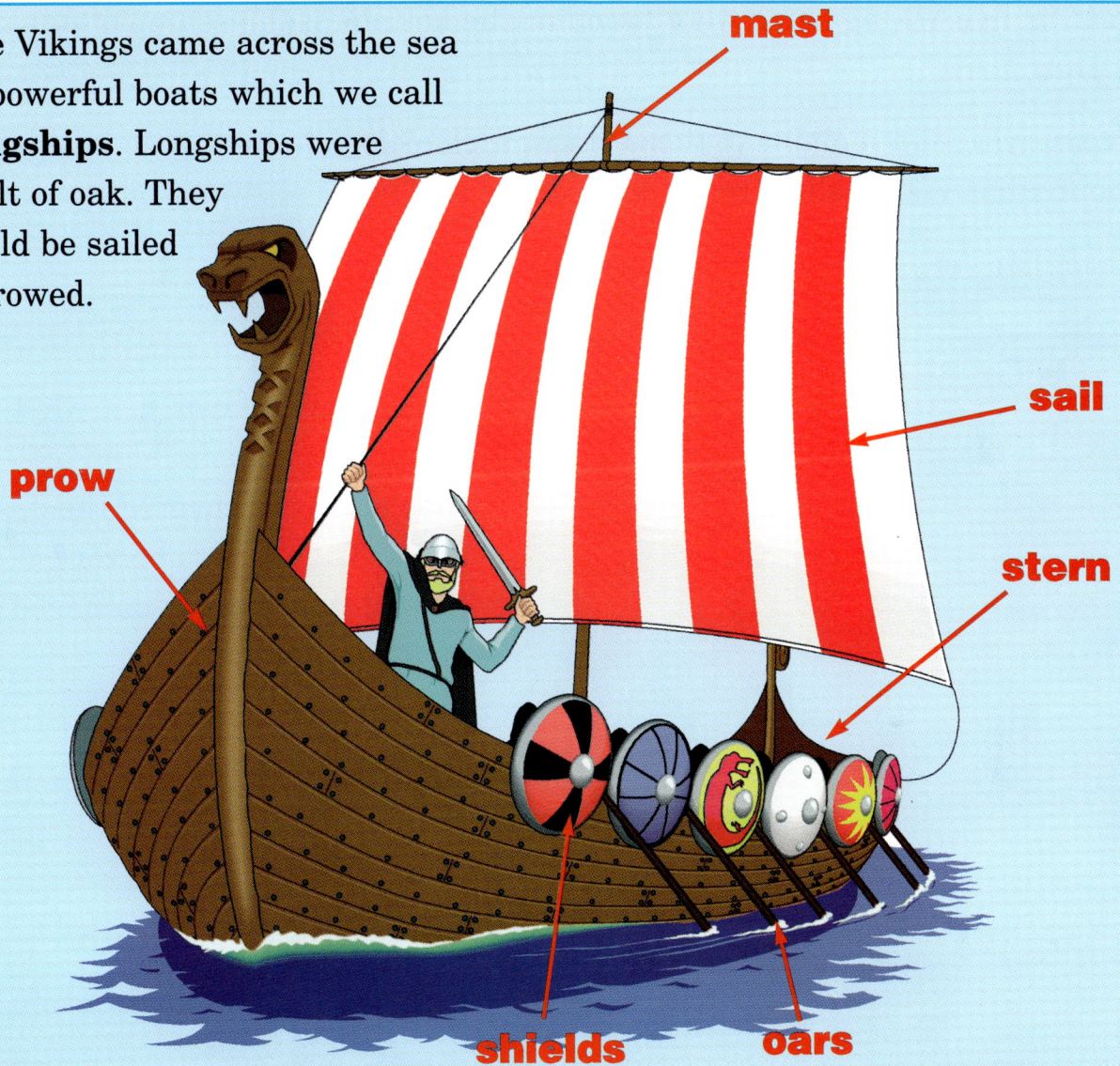

mast

sail

prow

stern

shields

oars

The front of a boat is called a **prow**. The Vikings often carved the prows of their longships into the shape of a fierce dragon. The Vikings believed that the sign of the dragon would protect them from storms at sea.

**longship, mast, sailed, rowed, prow.**

# Five Viking ships

In 1962 five Viking ships were found at the bottom of the sea near **Roskilde** in **Denmark**.

By studying the remains of these ships, archaeologists were able to learn about what Viking ships really looked like and how they were built.

This picture shows just what the archaeologists found as they slowly uncovered the ships. They had to be very careful in case they damaged anything.

Can you see the outline of a ship?

Here is the same ship, now put together and on show in the museum at Roskilde.

Some archaeologists then built modern copies of the Viking ships. They did this so that they could prove that these ships could really sail and travel long distances.

This is a picture of a full size copy of one of the Viking warships which was found in Denmark. It is called the *Helge Ask*.

# Navigation

The Vikings didn't have any maps or compasses to tell them how to get to different countries. So how did they find their way across the seas?

The Vikings navigated by noting the position of the sun, moon and stars. They could also look at wave formations, sea birds and floating objects to learn which direction the land was in.

How do you think that the position of the sun, moon and stars could help a Viking to navigate?

What things might the Vikings have found floating in the sea?

What might you find floating in the sea nowadays?

compass, navigation.

# Where did they go?

Vikings from different parts of Scandinavia went to different places.

The Norwegian and Danish Vikings headed west and south. They settled in France, Britain (which is England, Scotland and Wales all together), the Faroe Islands, Ireland, Greenland and Iceland.

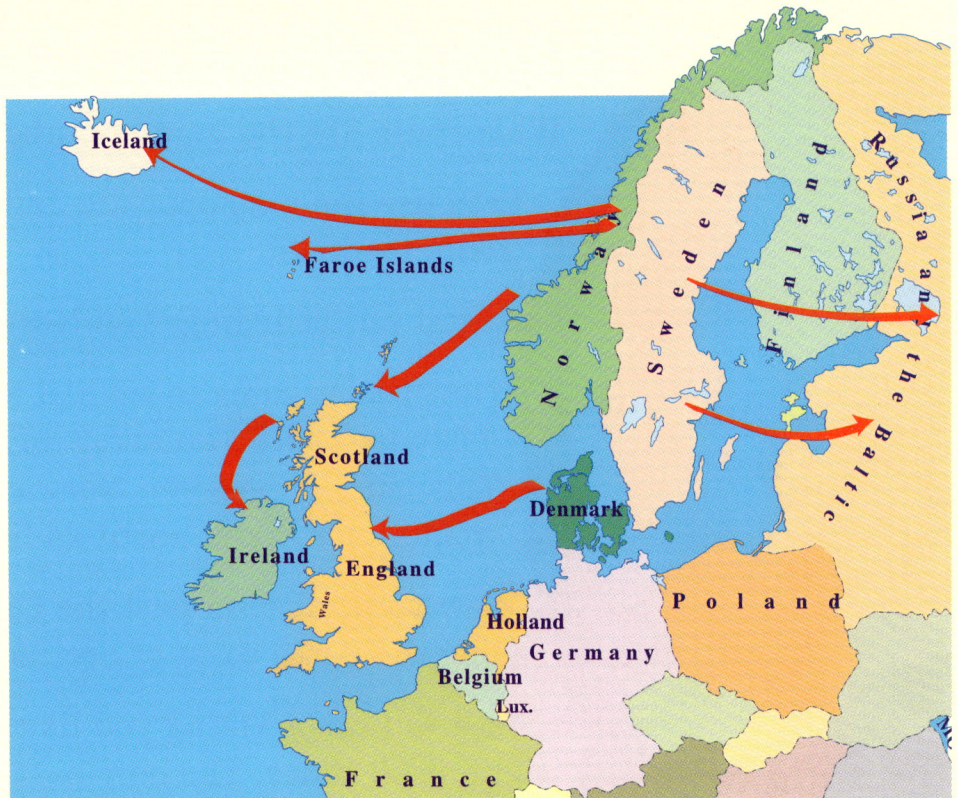

The Swedish Vikings headed east to the Baltic and Russia.

So, the Vikings who came to Britain and Ireland would have come from **Norway** and **Denmark**.

Look at the map. Find all the countries mentioned on this page.

But one of them is not on this map! Which one is it?

Use a globe to locate the missing country.

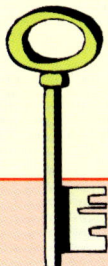

**Britain, settled, the Baltic, locate.**

# Their route to Britain and Ireland

Pretend that you are a Norwegian Viking. You have a boat full of furs and you want to go to Ireland to trade them.

What route are you going to take?

Let's use the map opposite and plan your sailing route together.

First put your finger on Norway.

Now you're going to set sail for the Shetland Islands. There's an arrow to show you the way. This journey between Norway and the Shetlands would have taken about 24 hours in good weather.

Now you travel on past the Orkney Islands and along the north coast of Scotland.

Since you are a Viking you like to keep the land in sight at all times. The only part of this journey where you were out of sight of land was when you sailed between Norway and Shetland.

Now you sail on, down the west coast of Scotland and head for the Irish coast.

Why do you think the Vikings liked to keep the land in sight when they were sailing?

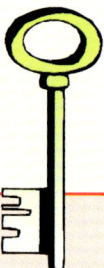

route.

ATLANTIC

OCEAN

Shetland
Islands

Orkney
Islands

Scotland

NORTH

SEA

England

Ireland

Wales

HOLLAND

BELGIUM

GERMANY

NORWAY

SWEDEN

BALTIC SEA

DENMARK

POLA

# The Vikings in Scotland

The first Viking attack on Scotland took place in 795. This was a raid on the island of **Iona** where there was a wealthy monastery. The Vikings settled mostly in the west of Scotland, particularly on the Scottish Islands.

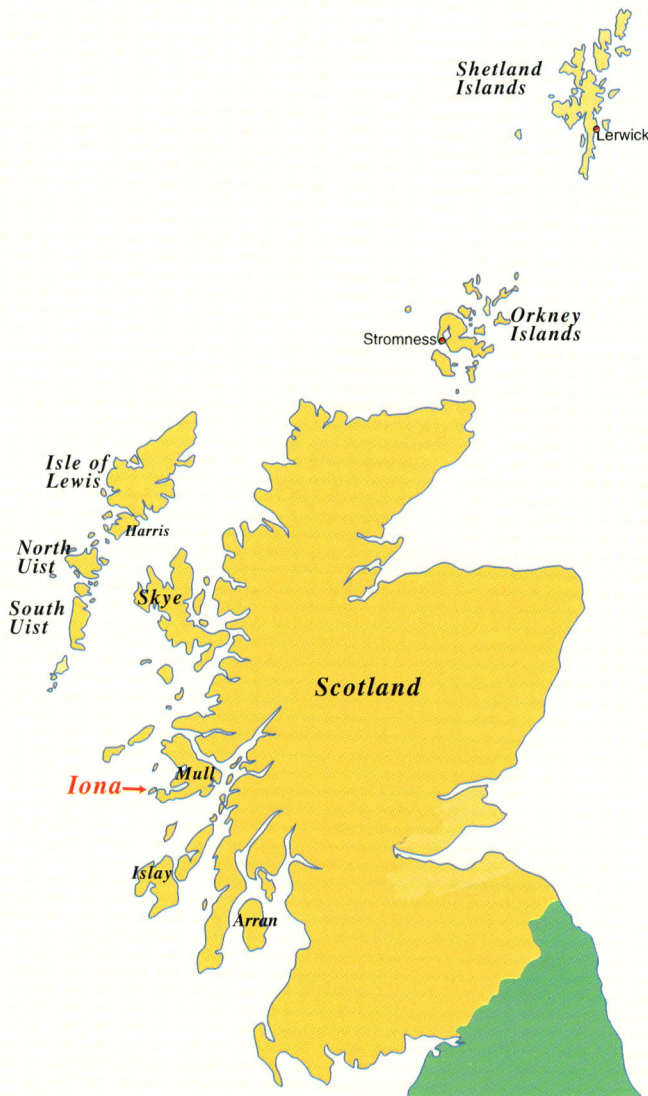

*Shetland Islands*

Lerwick

*Orkney Islands*

Stromness

*Isle of Lewis*

*Harris*

*North Uist*

*Skye*

*South Uist*

**Scotland**

*Mull*

**Iona**→

*Islay*

*Arran*

NORTH

Study these facts:

1  There were Vikings in Norway, Sweden and Denmark.

2  From about the year 800, there were Vikings in Scotland.

3  Ireland is very close to Scotland.

Which Vikings were most likely to attack Ireland?

**raid, wealthy.**

# When the Vikings arrived!

Some Vikings raided the areas that they visited and stole anything of value. Monasteries and surrounding settlements were plundered again and again.

From them they stole ornaments, jewellery, food and other valuable goods.

They also captured people and sold them into slavery.

But not all Vikings were thieves and fighters. In fact, most Vikings were much more interested in trading than they were in raiding.

This picture of the Viking raid on Nendrum was drawn in 1927. How old is the picture?

# Alfred the Great

The Vikings conquered much of the north-eastern part of the land which we now call England. This part was inhabited by people called **Angles** and **Saxons**. The part the Vikings conquered was called the **Danelaw** because the Vikings who lived there were Danes. The Vikings were winning many battles and it seemed as if they would soon have power over the whole country.

**Why were some Vikings called Danes?**

For many years the Saxons and the Vikings battled to decide who should rule the country. Then, in the year 871, a man called **Alfred** became king of the west Saxon kingdom. For his first few years as king, the Vikings won most of the battles. To defeat the Vikings, Alfred built many fortified towns called **burhs**. Some of these burhs were brand new towns, such as Oxford.

Other burhs were old towns to which he added new **fortifications**. Winchester was one of these towns.

He also decided to form a **navy**.

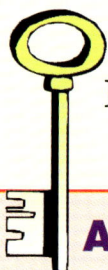

**Angles, Saxons, inhabited, Danelaw, navy, fortifications.**

Alfred helped the Saxon people to unite and fight back against the Vikings. It took seven years, but Alfred managed to conquer much of the Danelaw.

When Alfred died he was greatly missed. He was remembered as a good king because he cared about his people. He was a Christian and people call him **Alfred the Great**.

The **Anglo-Saxon Chronicles** are a record of all the important things that had happened in England up to the Middle Ages. They were written by monks.

This is what they said about the death of Alfred:

"**Alfred, the son of King Aethelwulf, passed away six nights before All Saints' Day. He was king over all the English, except for the part known as the Danelaw; and he ruled over his kingdom for twenty-eight years.**"

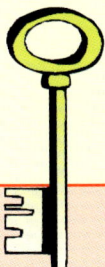

When is All Saints' Day?

**Chronicles, unite.**

Talk about how a king would show that he cared about his people.

On the board, make a list of the things you think of.

# York in Viking times

**York** is a town in the north of England. It was founded by the Romans hundreds of years before the Vikings came, but the Vikings made it one of their most important towns.

They captured the town in 866. It was already an important trading centre when the Vikings took it over.

The Vikings didn't call the town 'York'. Their name for it was '**Jorvik**'. The 'J' sounds like a 'Y' so 'Jorvik' is pronounced 'Yorvik'.

This picture shows a site in the middle of York where archaeologists have found the remains of a Viking settlement.

Look at a map of the British Isles and find York.

Could you prepare a one minute talk about Viking York?

# How do we know about the Vikings?

There are several different sources that tell us about the past.

**Annals** are one source of evidence. These were the records that monks and scholars wrote. Some were written at the time things happened. Others were written much later. We still have these annals today. We can read them to learn what these people said the Vikings did.

The monks who wrote the Anglo-Saxon Chronicles said this about the year the Vikings first raided Britain:

"In this year, terrifying omens were seen in the land of Northumbria, and the people were afraid. There were powerful whirlwinds, thunder and lightening, and dragons were seen flying in the sky. These signs were followed by a great famine, and later that same year, on January 8th, heathen men attacked and destroyed God's church at Lindisfarne through cruel robbery and slaughter."

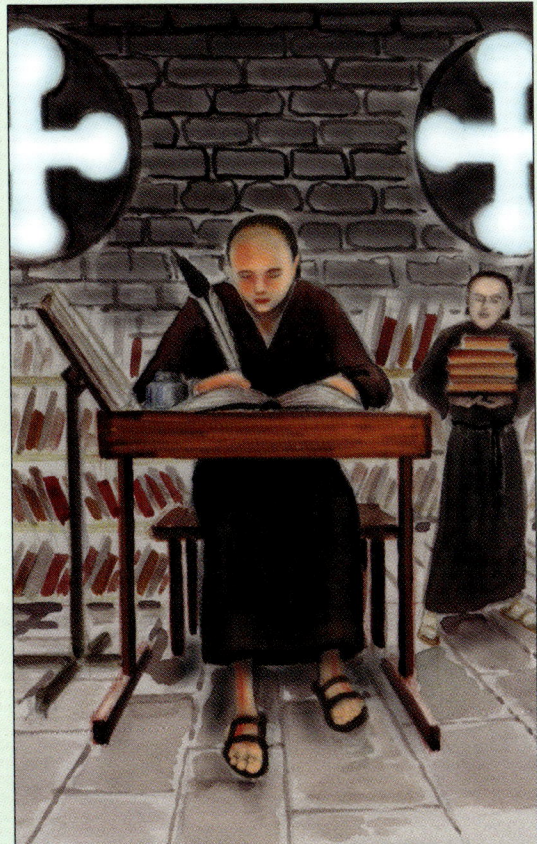

Who were the heathen men that the monks mentioned?

What do you think the Vikings thought of the monks?

source, annals, omen, heathen, famine, slaughter, scholars.

# Archaeology

**Archaeology** is another way of learning about the past.

Archaeologists study the buried remains of past times. Things like graves, weapons, coins, jewellery and the ruins of buildings can sometimes be found buried in the ground.

These archaeologists in York have found some Viking wood.

**What do you think this wood might have been part of?**

This Viking brooch was found in Dublin. It is called a **disc brooch**. Can you think why?

These are Viking keys which were found in York. They are made of iron.

**What do the items in both these pictures tell you about the Vikings?**

# Language and placenames

The language used by the Vikings is known as **Old Norse**. From this we get some of our words like 'market', 'penny', 'egg', 'knife', sky and 'window'.

'Fell' meaning a hill, and 'dale' meaning a valley are also Viking words.

We can tell where the Vikings settled by looking at placenames. Many placenames in Ireland are a mixture of Irish and Viking words. For example, 'Ballyholme' is made up of the Irish word 'baile' meaning a town or settlement, and the Viking word 'holme', meaning a meadow or flat place.

**Ballyholme**

**Carlingford**

Anywhere with a name that ends in '-by' was a Viking village, like Whitby in England. Anywhere with a name ending in 'haven' was a harbour, and a place with a name ending in 'wick' was a market. 'Ford' meant a narrow inlet — for example, Strangford means 'the ford of the strong current'.

**Keswick**

**Strangford**

'Land' is another Viking word. It means 'country'.

The names of the countries England ('land of the English'), Scotland ('land of the Scots'), and Ireland ('land of the Irish') were all made up by the Vikings.

**Scotland**

**Ireland**

**England**

# The runes

The Vikings wrote with letters called runes.

The runes were straight-edged letters with sharp corners. The Vikings didn't write on paper with a pen or pencil. Instead they carved the letters onto a piece of wood, stone, bone or sometimes metal.

Very few people knew how to write with runes, so if you knew how to write people were very impressed and thought that you were very clever.

The runes were used to write short messages or to name things. A Viking warrior might carve his name on his sword so that everyone would know who it belonged to.

This is a drawing of a rune-stone which was found at Blekinge in Scandinavia. It says "In memory of HariwulafR. HariwulafR, son of HaeriwulafR, cut these runes"

**Try to pronounce HariwulafR!**

Why do you think runes had straight edges and sharp corners?

There are no books written in runes. Why do you think this is?

# Turgeis

We are not sure that all the stories about the Vikings in Ireland are true. One story says that in Ireland there was a very bad Viking indeed. His name was **Turgeis** (pronounced *Tur-gice*) .

Turgeis was a Viking chieftain. He first came to Ireland in 832. He brought a large fleet with him and attacked the north of Ireland.

Some of Turgeis' ships went up the Bann to Lough Neagh. From there the Vikings made their way to Armagh.

In 840 Turgeis and his Viking followers attacked the great monastery at Armagh three times in one month. Turgeis chased the abbot and his monks out of the monastery.

Turgeis really wanted to take over the north of Ireland and rule it himself, but he did not succeed. In the year 845, he was taken prisoner by one of the kings of Ulster. Turgeis was drowned in Lough Owel as a punishment for all the trouble he had caused.

Who would have drowned Turgeis?

Write a story about the drowning of Turgeis. Start with his capture, then go on to his trial (if he had one) and what he was accused of, what he might have said, and end with his drowning.

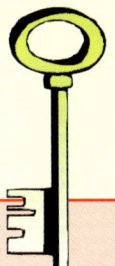

chieftain.

# Brian Boru

**Brian Boru** was an Irish king in the Viking age. He was born in what is now County Clare. You can read his story in a book called *Brian Boru* by Morgan Llywelyn.

Brian didn't like the Vikings. He wanted to force them out of Ireland. When he was a young man, he and his army of warriors fought and killed many Vikings in and around Limerick.

Brian's eldest brother was king of a large part of Ireland and when he died, Brian took his place. Because he was such a great leader, his kingdom grew. In 1002 he became **High King**. This meant that he was the most powerful king in Ireland.

He tried to persuade all the other Irish kings to join him in fighting against the Vikings.

I'm going to drive the Vikings out of Ireland.

I'm going to drive the Vikings from the land of the Saxons.

Here are the pictures of two kings and what they said. Talk about who they are. Which one of them lived first?

Discuss how these two kings were similar and how they were different.

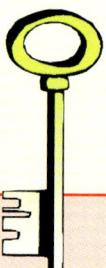

**force, High King, persuade.**

# The Battle of Clontarf

At Easter in 1014, a huge Viking army invaded Ireland, landing at **Clontarf**, near Dublin. They wanted to take over the whole of Ireland.

Brian Boru was old now and he could not fight, but he gathered a large army to fight the Vikings. He watched from his tent as about 8000 men took part in the battle.

The **Battle of Clontarf** was one of the biggest battles ever fought in Ireland.

The Irish won, but as the Vikings were running away, one of their chiefs, called **Brodir**, found Brian's tent. Brian was inside and Brodir ran in and killed him.

Brian Boru was buried at Armagh. If you go to the Church of Ireland cathedral in Armagh today, you can see a plaque near the spot where Brian's body is buried.

**cathedral, plaque.**

Talk about this picture. Who is the man with the sword? Who is the old man kneeling on the ground?

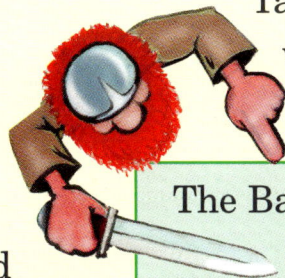

The Battle of Clontarf was a very important battle in Irish history. Write about how Brian Boru would have felt while this battle was going on. Use words like:

| | | |
|---|---|---|
| **fighting** | **dead** | **young** |
| **children** | **tent** | **friends** |
| **tired** | **watch** | **old** |

Make up a short play about the death of Brian Boru.

# Viking Dublin

In the early 1960s, builders found the remains of Viking Dublin buried in the ground next to the River Liffey. The builders were meant to be laying the foundations of a new office block on the site which was at **Wood Quay**.

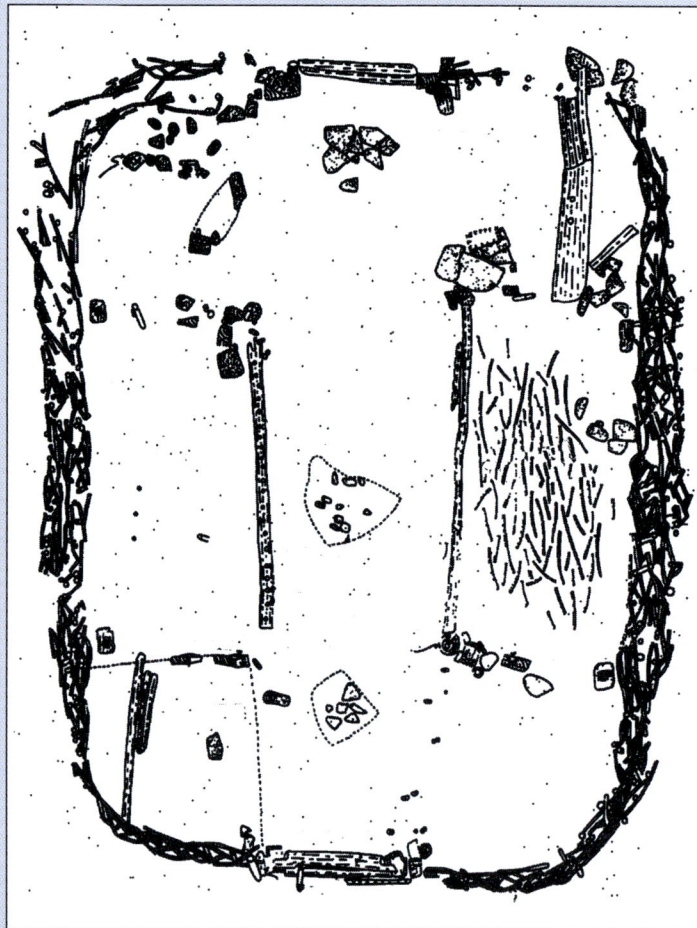

Here is a drawing of the remains of one of the houses which the archaeologists found in Dublin. Can you see the straw where the bed was? What might the other bits have been?

Archaeologists were allowed to dig and learn about the site before it was built on.

They found many Viking artifacts at Wood Quay, many of which are now in the National Museum in Dublin.

This is what a Viking house might have looked like.

Make a drawing of what your house looks like from the outside.

Now imagine that hundreds of years have gone by and archaeologists are digging in the area where you used to live. They might uncover the remains of your house! Make a drawing of your house like the one on page 34 to show what they might find and what might have disappeared.

# Viking markets

Most Vikings lived in small settlements where they made many of the things they needed.

Many of the great towns of Britain and Ireland that we know today, such as Dublin and York, began as Viking markets where people came to sell what they had made.

Other traders came with goods which they had brought from other countries. You will read about this on pages 38 and 39.

This woman is looking at the leather worker's stall in Jorvik.

Stalls like this were set out along the roadside and goods were displayed on wooden benches.

Think of all the things that a leather worker might make.

If the Vikings could make things like clothes and tools for themselves, why do you think they still went to the markets?

What other stalls might you find in a Viking market?

Even if you did not want to buy anything, why would it still be good to go to the market?

# How did they pay for things?

At the start of the Viking Age the Vikings didn't use money to pay for things. They didn't know what money was. They swapped things instead.

Later the Vikings learnt about money and began to use coins to pay for things.

One of these men is trying to swop a blanket for some grain. How much grain do you think he should get for one blanket?

This is a Viking coin that was found in Dundalk, Co Louth. It was made about 997 AD.

At first the Vikings swapped things to get what they wanted. Later they used money. Think about both ways and decide which way you think is better.

Perhaps you could try them out in class.

# What did the Vikings buy and sell?

Viking traders travelled great distances to buy goods which they could not get at home.

From Western Europe they bought sword blades, chain-mail coats, salt, wine, glass, pottery, and jewellery.

From Eastern Europe and Russia they bought silk, furs, spices, more glassware, drinking vessels, beads and precious stones.

They even got silk, spices and silver from as far away as Baghdad.

**SILVER**

From Russia they also got amber, wax and honey.

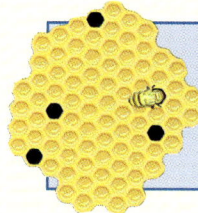

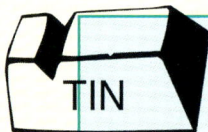

**TIN**

From Britain the Vikings got wheat, honey, silver, tin and goods made from wool.

Wool and falcons came from Iceland.

From the Middle East they bought silk, spices, wine, jewellery, brocade

Traders in their own Scandinavian countries were able to trade walrus tusks, furs, timber, bone combs and iron.

They also traded in slaves wherever they happened to be.

**brocade, precious stones, amber, falcons.**

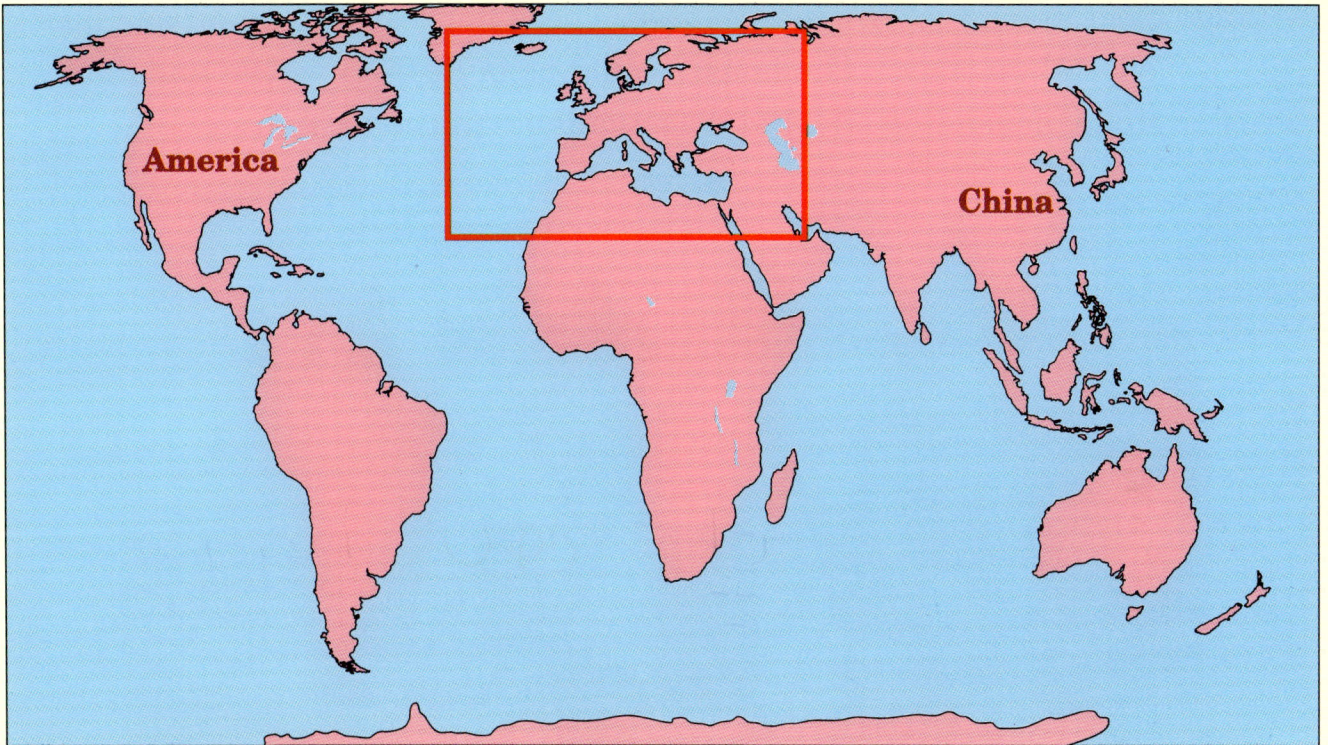

This red rectangle on this map shows you the area of the world where the Vikings traded.

You can see on the map how much of the world the Viking traders were able to reach.

Does this mean that they could never buy anything made in countries like China and America?

Can you think of a way they could get items from countries that the merchants couldn't travel to?

# Viking houses

Vikings lived in long rectangular houses. These houses were all on one floor (like a modern bungalow). The houses could be built from wattle and daub, wood or stone, depending on what was available in the local area.

## Discuss what is happening here.

**Clues:**

Hole in the ground

Surrounding screen

Bad smells

Handfuls of moss

There was one main room that was a kitchen, a living-room and a bedroom all rolled into one. Everyone slept in the same room.

There was a hearth for a fire in the centre of the main room, but there was no chimney and there were no windows, so the whole house would fill up with the smell of smoke.

Talk about what you can see in the picture above.

Use words like:

| | | |
|---|---|---|
| **smoke** | **bed** | **furniture** |
| **fire** | **clothing** | |
| **utensils** | **possessions** | |

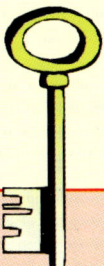

**wattle and daub, hearth.**

# Viking artifacts

The Vikings didn't have nearly as much furniture in their houses as we have in ours.

There was usually just one bed and the farmer and his wife slept there. Others in the family wrapped themselves in blankets or animal skins and lay on platforms around the walls.

Rugs and tapestries were hung on the walls to keep out draughts.

They had no wardrobes to hang their clothes in. They kept spare clothes in chests. Some of these chests could be locked if there was anything valuable like money or jewellery in them. On page 28 there is a picture of some keys which archaeologists found in York.

Food was kept in tubs and barrels made of wood and there would be some cooking utensils. The Vikings had knives and spoons but they didn't use forks.

They sat on stools or benches. A richer family might have some chairs.

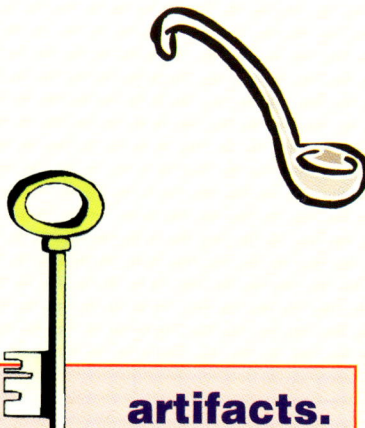

**artifacts.**

Talk about what it would be like to live in a Viking house.

Would it be like living in your house? What would be the same? What would be different?

# Vikings made cloth

The people in this picture are sitting beside a loom. Cloth is woven on a loom.

Write a story about this picture. Who do you think the people are and what might they be saying to each other? You might use words like:

| | | | |
|---|---|---|---|
| **wool** | **weaving** | **cloth** | **happy** |
| **spinning** | **mother** | **new clothes** | |

Think of all the things the Vikings might have made from cloth.

**loom, spinning, weaving.**

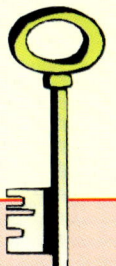

# Viking food

In Viking times there wasn't the same big choice of food that there is today. There were no fizzy drinks, no crisps, no beefburgers and no chocolate.

Vikings ate roasted and boiled meat, fish, bread, gruel, vegetables, fruits, berries, nuts, and drank wine and beer.

They loved to have feasts to which they invited all their friends. The women cooked and served the food, but they did not eat with the men.

Talk about the way the meat is being cooked. Use words like:

**spit     roast     fire     turning**

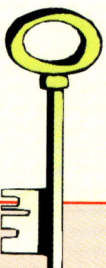

**gruel, spit.**

On board ship during a journey, the Vikings would have drunk water, beer or milk. These drinks would be stored in bags made from animal skins. The milk would have gone a bit sour during the journey. They would have eaten fish, bread and oat biscuits. Meat and fish could be preserved by salting, smoking, drying or pickling. Sometimes the food went bad.

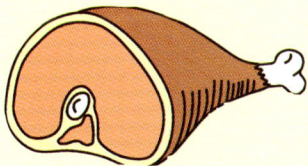

What sicknesses could the Vikings have suffered from on a sea journey?

What would have caused them?

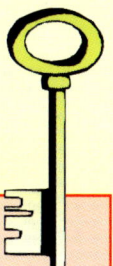

**preserved, salting, smoking, drying, pickling.**

# Viking clothes

Men and boys would have worn a tunic with a pair of trousers. They put on a cloak when they went out in the cold. Cloaks were worn with the opening to the side of the sword arm. This left the sword arm free for fighting.

Woman and girls wore ankle-length dresses of wool or linen with a pinafore over the top. The pinafore was fastened at the shoulders with large brooches.

Here are a Viking man and boy.

What three weapons is the man carrying?

The Vikings had coloured cloth. Can you think how they coloured it?

Here are some words to give you a clue!

**plants    roots
berries    dye
leaves**

Both men and women wore jewellery. They wore brooches, bracelets and necklaces, but not earrings. They did not use buttons very often and zips had not been invented, so clothes were fastened with large pins, brooches and belts.

Vikings liked to keep very clean. They were particularly fussy about keeping their hair clean and tidy. Huge numbers of Viking combs have been found, which shows how many Vikings carried combs around with them to keep their hair neat.

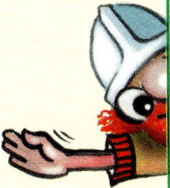

Here are a Viking woman and girl.

Do you think these are rich people or poor people?

Talk about the items lying around them. What do you think they are?

# Armour

When Vikings went on a raid or into battle they wore armour.

They wore helmets which had neck guards and nose guards.

They also wore chain-mail to protect themselves.

helmet

noseguard

chain mail
glove

wristguard

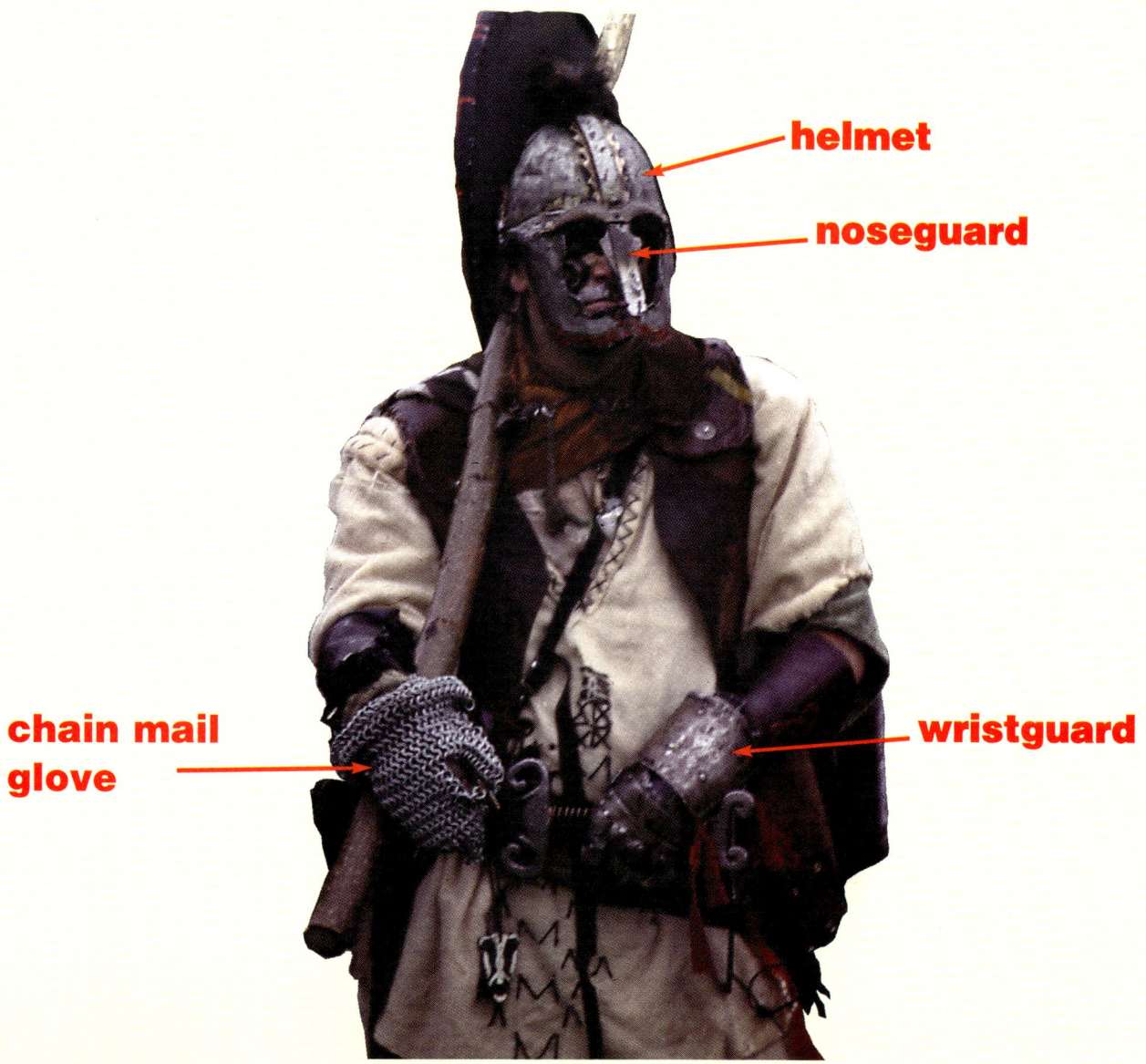

Discuss what each of the items of armour is for.

What might this warrior wear under his tunic?

# Weapons

Vikings fought with swords, with axes, with spears, with javelins, and with bows and arrows.

A Viking protected himself with a round shield. He would paint his shield bright colours.

Shields were made of wood.

javelin.

Imagine you are a Viking warrior and have to design a shield for yourself.

Get a really big piece of paper and draw a large circle. Now draw or paint the pattern you would like on your shield.

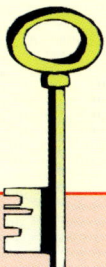

# Viking men

Because the Vikings went to sea so much, many of the men spent a lot of time on their ships, even when they weren't sailing.

In this picture you can see some men working around their ship, getting it ready for its next voyage.

One man is mending a sail; another is loading on barrels. I wonder what the boy on the right is doing.

**? What do you think might be in the barrels?**

Some men never went to sea.

When Viking men were at home they could spend their time farming, hunting and fishing or making tools and weapons.

A man who was a servant might be expected to stay on the farm and work when his master was away.

Viking men could also be blacksmiths, leather-workers or craftsmen.

Talk about the work of the blacksmith and leather worker.

Which of these things would have been made by a leather-worker and which would have been made by a blacksmith?

**sword   boots   shoes   spear-head   satchel   helmet**

# Viking women

Viking women did not go on raids or go sailing. They stayed at home. They had very important jobs to do.

The women looked after the farm while their husbands, fathers, brothers and sons were away. They made sure that the slaves knew what to do. As well as organising others, they did the sewing and weaving, cooked and looked after the children.

Discuss what sort of person a Viking wife had to be.

What skills did she need?

# Viking children

Viking children were expected to grow up quickly.

The boys were taught how to hunt, sail and fight.

The girls were taught to sew, weave and cook.

This is a Viking toy boat which was found in Winetavern Street, in Dublin.

Viking children had some toys, although they didn't have the same choice as there is today. They could have toy horses, toy ships and pretend swords and shields.

They also had board games, nursery rhymes and songs.

This is a board from a game which the Vikings played.

There are holes in it, and there is a central hole with a ring around it.

Can you make up a game which might be played on this board?

Why were boys taught to hunt, sail and fight?

Why were girls taught to sew, weave and cook?

# Pastimes

In the evening the Vikings would all sit around together and:

     feast

     tell stories

     sing

     play  music

     play board games

     sleep

Write down all the things you do in the evening.

Now compare your list with what the Vikings did.

Are any activities the same? Are any activities different?

# Sagas

While they were gathered around the fireside the Vikings loved to listen to stories. The Vikings had special stories called sagas. A saga was a tale of heroic deeds done by a great person. A saga was often based on a true story, but the story-teller could add more bits to make it more exciting.

Here is **Runolf** the story-teller. He is telling the story of **Sigurd**.

Here is part of it:

"Long, long ago, a boy was born to **King Sigmund** and he was named Sigurd. When he became a young man he was sent to live with old **Regin** the blacksmith who taught him all the crafts that he would need to be a great leader.

One day, Regin called Sigurd to him and told him of a great treasure owned by the **Nibelungs**, hidden in a cave guarded by a giant called **Fafnir**. Sigurd decided that he would go in search of the treasure. Calling the great horse **Greyfell** to him, he set off to say farewell to his mother. All she could give him was the sword of his dead father. Sadly, it was broken but Sigurd knew the very man who could restore it. Such was the skill of Regin that the repaired sword was able to split a mighty anvil without being harmed. So sharp was it that even a strand of soft wool blown against its edge was cut in two.

Sigurd rode until he came to a forest where Fafnir, disguised as a fierce dragon, challenged him. Straight to the heart of the dragon went the sword of Sigurd and the great beast screamed in its death throes. As he drew his hand across his mouth Sigurd tasted the dragon's blood that had splashed over him. From that moment he could understand the language of the birds. They told him exactly where to find the treasure and very soon, Sigurd had riches beyond his wildest dreams."

Make up a short play based on this story and act it out in class. Remember you can add bits to the story if you like!

You could also draw pictures of some of the things that happened.

# Religion

Did you know that two of the days of our week are named after Thor and Freya?

Guess which days they are!

Can you find out the names of more Viking gods and what the Vikings believed about them?

The Vikings were pagan. They believed in many gods and goddesses.

The Vikings believed that each of their gods looked after a different part of their lives.

For example, there was **Thor**, god of thunder and war and **Freya**, goddess of love.

The Vikings would make sacrifices of animals and people to their gods. They believed that this kept their gods happy.

This man is dressed up as **Odin**. The Vikings thought he was the most powerful god of all.

**god, goddess, sacrifice.**

# The Vikings became Christians

When the Vikings travelled overseas, either to fight or to trade, they met people whose religion was Christianity. You have already learnt how they attacked monasteries in Ireland.

They got to know about this religion and they saw how rich some of the Christian kings and monasteries were. It must have seemed as if the Christian god was powerful.

As they settled in other countries, they began to marry Christians. Perhaps their children would be brought up as Christians. The Christian members of the household would influence the others.

In the year 1000, the Vikings in Iceland took a vote on what religion they should be. Half wanted to change to Christianity and half wanted to keep their old gods. Finally, the leader chose Christianity but said that it would be all right for people to worship their old gods in secret!

As trade with Christian merchants increased, it became easier to do business if you were the same religion as they were. Many Vikings became Christians because of this, but still believed in their old gods as well.

# Viking art

This is the head of a battle-axe. Someone has spent a long time decorating this!

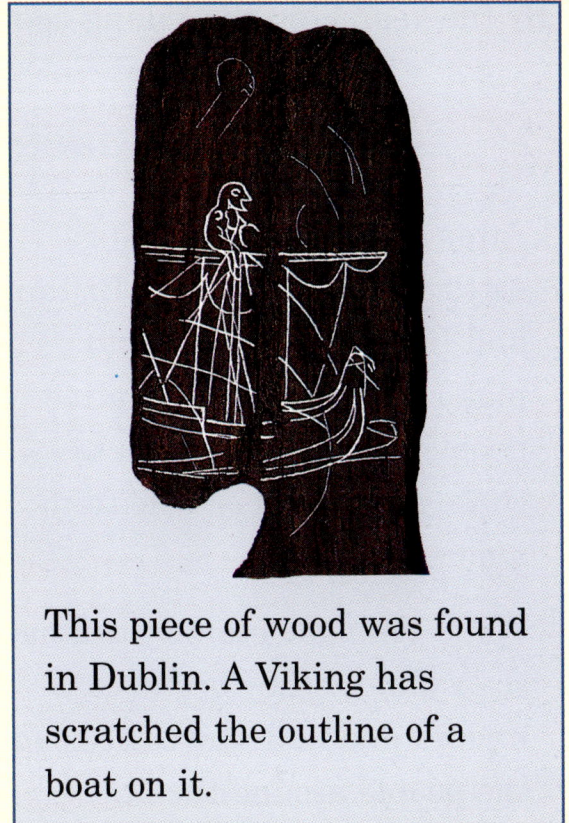

This piece of wood was found in Dublin. A Viking has scratched the outline of a boat on it.

Vikings loved to decorate things around them.

They liked to paint pictures of animals and the gods.

They would draw and paint designs on all sorts of things: on their houses, on stones, on furniture, on weapons and on shields.

They also made decorative metalwork. On page 28 you saw a decorated metal brooch.

It took lots of skill and many years of practice to be able to draw like this.

decorative.

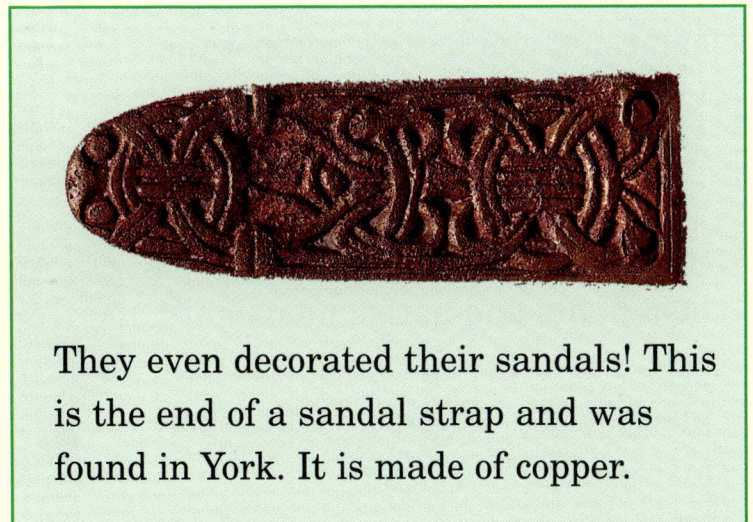

They even decorated their sandals! This is the end of a sandal strap and was found in York. It is made of copper.

# Why did the Viking Age end?

By the year 1100 the Viking age was over.

## Look at these facts:

1 After a while, when Vikings settled in lands such as Britain and Ireland, they began to make friends with the native people and perhaps even to chose a husband or wife from amongst them.

2 Some Vikings became Christians and so gradually they began to understand and share the religion of the people around them.

3 More good land was cultivated in Scandinavia and so it was not necessary for a young man to go to another country to set up his own farm.

4 Rulers in Europe had better armies and could win battles against the Vikings, who found it very difficult to attack the new stone castles. It was now better for the Vikings to trade with other people. So Viking merchants and native merchants began to share the same trading places which became towns where everyone mixed together.

Take each of the facts on the left one by one and talk about how each of them helped to bring the Viking age to an

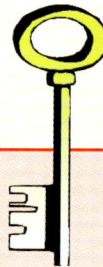

**native, cultivated, merchants**

# The Battle of Stamford Bridge

In Norway there was a Viking who had relatives who had once ruled England. He was called **Harald Hardrada**. In 1066, he took a large Viking army and tried to conquer England. His army sailed up the River Humber and captured York.

The king of England at this time was **Harold Godwinson**. He took his army all the way from London to York to fight the Vikings. He beat them at the **Battle of Stamford Bridge** on 25 September 1066.

King Harold and his army then had to race all the way back to the south coast because *another* army was invading!

Imagine you are a soldier in King Harold's army. Tell the story of leaving London to march north and what happens to you.

You could start something like this: "We were resting in London when King Harold told us that ...".

Talk about the things an army needs when it is marching and fighting. Use words like:

**food, water, danger, tired, sick, excited, hurt, killed, weapons, feet**

The green arrows on this map show you the journey of Harold's army from London to Stamford Bridge and back to the south coast.

The purple arrows show where the new invaders were coming from. The little crossed swords show where the battles were.

# The Normans invade Britain

The new invaders were called Normans. Their name comes from 'Northmen', because they had come from the north and settled in France.

In fact, their ancestors were Vikings from Scandinavia.

**ancestors.**

King Harold and his army fought the Normans at the **Battle of Hastings** in October, **1066**. The leader of the Normans was called William. Harold and his men were very tired after the Battle of Stamford Bridge and the long march south. Harold was killed at the Battle of Hastings and his army was defeated.

The **Bayeux Tapestry** is a very famous piece of embroidered cloth. It is very long and the pictures tell the story of William conquering England.

This part of it shows Harold being killed at the Battle of Hastings.

Can you make out Harold's name? 'Rex' means 'king'.

Not everyone agrees which soldier is Harold. Which one do you think he is?

Where do your parents come from? Where did your grand-parents and great grand-parents come from? Can you go any further back in time?

What have you found out? Where did *your* ancestors come from?

The Normans then conquered England — but that's *another* story ...

# Facts about the Vikings

1. They came from Denmark, Norway and Sweden.

2. They started to come to Britain and Ireland in the 790's.

3. Only Norwegian and Danish Vikings came to Britain and Ireland.

4. They came in powerful ships called longships.

5. They were strong warriors.

6. They raided monasteries and stole anything of value.

7. They took people prisoner and sold them as slaves.

8. They first raided England at Lindisfarne in 793.

9. They first raided Scotland in 795 at Iona.

10. The first Viking raid on Ireland was on Rathlin Island in 795.

11. Europe and Russia were also raided.

12. Later they learnt to trade.

13. They settled in many important towns like Dublin and York.

14. They settled in Northern Ireland.

15. The Viking women stayed at home and looked after the farm while the men were away.

16. They used an alphabet of letters called runes.

17. They believed in many gods.

18. Later many of them became Christians.

19. They spoke a language we call Old Norse.

20. The last Viking battle in England was the Battle of Stamford Bridge in 1066.

# Glossary

| | |
|---|---|
| agriculture | farming |
| Alfred the Great | a king of England. He helped the Saxons to unite and fight back against the Vikings. He was a Christian and people thought he was a very good king. |
| annals | the records that monks kept. They recorded the events that were happening, like a history book. |
| archaeology | the study of buried remains. Things from the past can be found buried in the ground. These things can be studied to help us learn about the past. |
| Christianity | Belief in God as explained to us by Jesus. |
| conquer | to win a war, to get control over something, eg a country. |
| convent | a building where nuns live. |
| Danelaw | the part of England that was taken over by Danish Vikings. |
| fertile | land which can produce good crops. |
| invader | someone who attacks a country. |
| longship | a Viking warship. |
| loom | a frame on which thread is woven into cloth. |

# Glossary

| | |
|---|---|
| mast | a long upright pole made for carrying the sail on a ship. |
| monastery | a building where monks live. |
| navigation | planning a safe journey across the sea. |
| Old Norse | the language that the Vikings spoke. |
| paganism | a belief in many gods. |
| plunder | to attack, destroy and steal. |
| prow | the front of a ship. |
| raid | a speedy attack on an enemy. |
| ringfort | an Irish fortified homestead in pre-Viking times. |
| runes | the letters used by the Vikings. |
| saga | a long story about a Viking hero. |
| Scandinavia | Denmark, Norway and Sweden, the Viking homelands. |
| settler | someone who leaves the country they were born in, and goes to live in a new country. |
| trader | someone who makes his living by buying and selling goods; also called a merchant. |

# Notes

The following are just a few of the many places of interest connected with the Vikings.

## Northern Ireland

The Ulster Museum
Botanic Gardens
BELFAST
BT9 5AB
Tel: 01232 383000

Down County Museum
The Mall
Downpatrick
Co Down
BT30 6AH
Tel: 01396 615218

## Republic of Ireland

The National Museum of Ireland
Kildare Street
DUBLIN 2
Tel: 01 (from NI- 003531) 6777444

Dublinia
St Michael's Hill
Christ Church
DUBLIN 8
Tel: 01 (from NI- 003531) 6794611

## England

The British Museum
Great Russell Street
LONDON
WC1B 3DG
Tel: 0171 6361555

Jorvik Viking Centre
Coppergate
YORK
YO1 1NT
Tel: 01904 643211

### Scotland
The Royal Museum of Scotland
Chambers Street
Edinburgh
EH1
Tel: 0131 2257534

Vikingar!
Barrfields
Greenock Road
Largs
North Ayrshire
Tel: 01475 689777

The following is a list of novels about Viking times, written for children. Not all of them are in print, but most should be available through libraries.

*The Bell of Nendrum* J S Andrews

*The Conquering Ships* B Bartos Hoppiner

*Horned Helmet* M de Angeli

*The Saga of Eric the Viking* T Jones

*Beyond the Dragon Prow* R Leeson

*The Viking Princess* and *Sea Wolves of the North* M Mullum

*The Sea King* M Pinder

*Odin's Monster* S Price

*Children of the Vikings* J Rumbold

*Astrid the Dark Eyed* J Salvesen

*Hengest's Tale* J P Walsh

*Brian Boru* Morgan Llywelyn

*Murtagh and the Vikings* M Morpurgo

By Henry Treece:

*Viking's Dawn*

*The Burning of Njal*

*Vinland the Good*

*Viking's Sunset*

*The Road to Miklagard*

*The Last of the Vikings*